DON'T GET RAILROADED™

A Railroad Worker's Guidebook to Protecting Yourself After Your Injury

Insider Tips From A Trusted Attorney

Carisa German-Oden, Esq.

Poolson Oden | www.PoolsonOden.com

Copyright © 2019, Poolson Oden

All rights reserved. No part of this book may be used or reproduced in any manner whatsoever without written permission of the author.

Printed in the United States of America.

ISBN: 9781699888612

DISCLAIMER:

This book is meant for informational purposes only. The legal statutes mentioned in this book were current as of the publication date, however, we cannot guarantee that these statutes have remained the same since the publication date. The information contained herein is not intended, and should not be taken, as legal advice. You are advised to contact a railroad attorney for counsel on particular issues and concerns. Additionally, your use or request of our materials does not constitute as an attorney-client relationship between you and the Poolson Oden Firm.

Contents

DON'T GET RAILROADED™ I

RAILROAD CLAIMS 1

WHAT CAN I RECOVER AFTER MY
RAILROAD INJURY?... 5

HOW DOES THE RAILROAD CLAIM PROCESS
WORK IN COURT?... 8

DEALING DIRECTLY WITH THE RAILROAD
CLAIMS DEPARTMENT.. 18

RETURNING TO WORK AFTER AN
INJURY CLAIM... 24

FELA: FAQS:.. 30

WHISTLEBLOWER FRSA FAQS:....................... 40

FINAL THOUGHTS 44

ABOUT POOLSON ODEN 44

WWW.POOLSONODEN.COM

RAILROAD CLAIMS THE BASICS

As a railroad worker, when you get hurt at work you have very different rights than other people working in most other industries. Your railroad injury is covered by a Federal law called the Federal Employers Liability Act, or FELA for short. This is the law that covers your injuries and it requires that the railroad provide you with 'a safe place to work' and holds the railroad responsible for your injury if the railroad caused or contributed to your accident. The railroad has to 'make you whole' and put you back to where you should have been before your injury if your railroad caused or contributed to your injury, even in the slightest. This is very, very different than workers' compensation laws, and it can help you recover a tremendous amount more in settlement or in court for your claim.

> FELA ► Federal Employers Liability Act ► law requiring railroad to provide you with 'a safe place to work' and holds the railroad responsible for your injury if the railroad caused or contributed to your accident.

Under the FELA which covers your injury rights, there is a special section called the Federal Safety Appliance Act. This part of the FELA requires that the railroad ensure that parts of the railcars and engines are safe, including the couplers, hand brakes, locomotive brakes, running boards, and sill steps. If your injury was caused even in part by defective equipment, the railroad may have violated the Safety Appliance Act. When the railroad violates this Act, and the violation leads to your injury, the railroad is absolutely liable. This means that the railroad cannot argue to a jury that you have done something wrong.

> Federal Safety Appliance Act ▶ part of FELA requiring the railroad to ensure that parts of the railcars and engines are safe.
>
> Federal Rail Safety Act ▶ protects you reporting your own injury, asking for medical treatment due to your injury, and reporting an unsafe condition at work that may have lead to the injury.

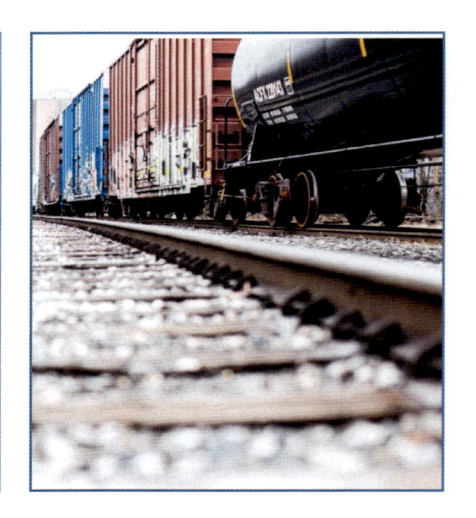

Finally, as a railroad worker you are also protected by the Federal Rail Safety Act (FRSA). The FRSA has real teeth in it and it protects you in the following situations:

- reporting your own injury to the railroad

- asking for medical treatment due to your own injury

- reporting an unsafe condition at work, that may have lead to your accident or that you simply may have noticed while working.

If the railroad violates the FRSA you are entitled to any actual damages you suffered including back pay, front pay if its best for you not to return to work, emotional damages you may have suffered, attorney fees for you, and even up to $250,000 in punitive damages. Many railroad workers have heard this law called the whistleblower statute, but we think that may give the law an unfair name. There is no shame in reporting an accident or unsafe condition at your railroad, or in demanding proper medical treatment. Some may feel the term whistleblower means someone who 'turns' on the company — we feel that making the railroad safer is the best thing you can do for yourself and your fellow workers.

WWW.POOLSONODEN.COM

WHAT CAN I RECOVER AFTER MY RAILROAD INJURY?

There are basically three laws that protect you after your injury: FELA (the most basic and most broad federal law); the Safety Appliance Act (applies if your injury was caused by a defective appliance on the train; and FRSA (applies if your railroad tries to 'strong arm' you into not reporting your accident, a safety violation or tries to deny or delay medical treatment to you after your injury).

Making an injury claim under the FELA allows you to seek the following damages:

- pain and suffering, both physical as well as emotional, and both past and any future pain that may be expected.

- wages, past lost wages and any future wages you may lose if you cannot return to work for the railroad.

- fringe benefits and lost retirement income.

- medical expenses, past and any future expenses you may need down the road.

Please read the above list again carefully since it shows how valuable your FELA claim may be. **If you suffer an injury that makes it unlikely you can return to work on the railroad, and the railroad bears some responsibility for your injury, then you may be entitled to a tremendous amount of money from your railroad.**

If your injury was caused by a defective handbrake or other safety appliance, it is important that you speak with an attorney familiar with railroad equipment and its uses so that a claim can be made under the FELA for this defect. Although the Safety Appliance Act does not provide for any extra damages beyond those listed above for FELA, it could make it easier to win you case in court or to receive a larger settlement.

Finally, if the railroad tried to bully you after you reported your injury or they made it hard for you to get medical treatment, you may be able to also file a claim under the whistleblower statute, in addition to FELA/Safety Appliance Act claim(s). You can possibly get extra damages under the whistleblower statute including attorney fees and up to $250,000 in punitive damages if your railroad was blatant in harassing you after an injury or blacklisting you when holding the railroad accountable for your safety.

All of this may sound complicated, but it's not. Our office focuses on railroad claims and I have spent my entire 17-year legal career focusing on helping railroad workers. Our firm will easily be able to help you navigate through the claims you should file to best protect yourself and maximize your recovery.

HOW DOES THE RAILROAD CLAIM PROCESS WORK IN COURT?

Railroad clients often ask us how their injury claim works. Do they have to file a claim in court immediately, when is the last day that they can file in court, and how long does the claim process take once it is filed in court?

Before discussing the 'written' deadlines by which you must get your claim filed in court or you lose all of your rights, a few comments about the court set deadlines. These are not meant to serve as any sort of guideline for when you should actually file your claim in court. The court deadlines are simply the final cut off dates— the last possible date after which you lose all your rights. So why would a person want to file a claim in court before the absolute last day the law allowed? Several reasons.

First, the sooner you file your claim in court, the sooner your claim will be resolved by the railroad for the most fair amount possible. Look at it this way— you suffer an injury at work; your doctors explain to you that you have a bad injury and it will likely keep you from returning to work full duty; 12 months have now gone by since your accident; you know that if you can't return to work you will lose at least $1 million in future wages and benefits, not to mention money for your pain and suffering; the railroad doesn't quite see it that way.... When you approach the railroad, they decide to offer $100,000 and explain that they think that is a very fair offer.

This is the important thing to understand—

the railroad knows you have no bargaining or negotiation power—you can't force them to go to an upcoming trial because you haven't even filed your claim yet.

From the railroad's point of view, they can simply put your claim on the back-burner and wait you out until

1. you now find an attorney who handles railroad claims (not many attorneys know how to handle such claims),

2. you file your claim in court,

3. your claim gets a trial date (likely 10 to 12 months away), and

4. the trial date actually approaches and is in the near future. The railroad can then simply re-visit your claim and decide how much to really offer you at that time.

Compare that to filling a claim in court within a month or two of knowing that

1) you suffered an injury at work that was in part the railroad's fault, and

2) you need medical treatment and it's possible you won't be able to return to work.

In that situation you will have a trial date set for around the time you are trying to settle your claim with the railroad. If the railroad isn't fair with you in settlement, then they know you will simply go to court and try your claim. This is what gets the railroad to pay the most in a settlement to you - the worry of a higher judgment in court if the claim can't be resolved before an upcoming trial. While there are always exceptions, we tell clients in general the best time to try to settle your claim with the railroad is as your trial date approaches. The second best time is after your claim is filed in court and the railroad knows you are serious. The worst time is before you have even filed a claim in court or maybe haven't even hired an attorney yet. From the railroad's eyes, you simply have no leverage until you have filed your claim in court.

Another reason filing your claim in court can be so important relates to the power of the court. Often the railroad tries to play games with your medical treatment and does not pay the bills as they are required to do under your collective bargaining agreement. If your claim is filed in court, it may be possible to have the court order the railroad to pay for medical treatment for you as is required. Or, more common, the railroad is certainly not going to hand over to you all the key documents in your claim such as the accident reports and the statements they may have taken from your co-workers, or evidence of any repairs or changes that may have been made after your injury. These documents and evidence can win a great settlement for you, but you will never know they are out there unless you file a claim in court. The court system simply levels the playing field and takes your claim out of the railroad's hands and puts it into the neutral hands of the court. When you file your claim in court all you are saying to the railroad is "Nothing personal, but this is extremely important to me, so let's bring in this neutral party to make sure we both behave."

One final thought on the court set deadlines for filing your railroad claim. Did you know that studies have been done that show if a company gives a very long 'free returns' period when they sell their product, it is less likely that buyers will return the product than if they are given a shorter 'free return' period? Yep, if you have 12 months to use something and you can still return it, no questions asked, you are much less likely to return it than if you only have a short 30 day period to try the product. It is human nature to think, "well, I have a lot of time left... I can return it next week or the week after." But we all delay until we forget or the product is damaged and we can't return it, even if we didn't even like it to begin with! Sometimes a very long window of time will run against our best interest since it makes it less likely we will take fast, decisive action.

    Now that you know why it's important to file your claim in court early, let's discuss the legal deadlines for filing railroad claims. Under FELA, workers have three years to bring an injury claim. Under the FRSA Whistleblower Statute, however, a railroad worker only has only 180 days, which is six months, to bring a claim. That timeframe is very short, and it's important that you talk to an attorney immediately to make sure that you don't miss your deadline to file a claim under the FRSA Whistleblower Statute. Remember, you have extra damages you may be able to get under the FRSA that you can't

WWW.POOLSONODEN.COM

get under FELA including attorney's fees and punitive damages!

For an injury claim, railroad workers are able to file their case in either state court or federal court. Because the law that protects railroad workers is a federal law, railroad workers have the choice to go to federal court. It's a decision that you will make with your attorney, and your attorney should be able to sit down and talk to you about the best court in which to file your claim. You will get a jury when you file an injury claim in either federal court or state court.

Many workers ask us how long the process takes. We all want things done 'yesterday' and your claim is no exception. You didn't ask to get hurt at work, and we understand that one of the many feelings you may be having is simply to get this over with as quickly as possible. But your claim is extremely important to you and it's very important it is handled correctly. This means getting medical testing done on any part of your body that may have been injured. You want to find out the full nature and extent of any injuries you may have suffered so that you can hold the railroad responsible for their role in your accident. This medical testing, and treatment, can take time. So while the court process itself does take time, understand that you are also getting medical treatment and testing done (which is certainly in your best interest), and all of this simply takes some amount of time. Any attorney that is being honest with you does not have a crystal ball to give you an exact timeline on how long your case will take— cases are different depending on the injuries involved and the court the claim is filed in.

As a general guideline most cases take from 10 to 16 months, but often a case can be settled for a fair amount after 8 to 12 months when all key documents have been obtained, witnesses have been deposed, and your medical injuries have been fully explored and identified. We like to tell clients, "Remember that the legal part of your case always follows the medical." What that means is it's hard to evaluate your case without making sure that we understand the severity and/or permanency of your injuries, which will be determined by your doctors. You would never want to have an attorney evaluate your claim while you're still treating for your injuries.

DEALING DIRECTLY WITH THE RAILROAD CLAIMS DEPARTMENT

Why It's Probably Not A Smart Way To Go!

Many injured railroad workers unfortunately believe that it may be easier to simply deal directly with the railroad's claims department in trying to resolve their claim. However, dealing with a railroad claims department puts an injured worker at risk of taking less, and often much less, for a settlement of their injury than what it is actually worth.

So why would you get less when you deal directly with the railroad? Let's take a step back and understand what makes up the 'value' of your claim; why does your railroad, or any railroad, pay money on a railroad injury claim?

First, why your accident happened is important. The more at fault the railroad is in causing your accident, the more of your 'total damages' they owe you. Well, if you deal directly with the railroad, you will not have access to the witness statements or investigative reports or pictures that may have been taken after your accident. You won't have the 'evidence' to wave in front of the railroad to say 'look, this is why you are at fault…and this is why you are at fault…'. As very experienced railroad attorneys, we routinely hire safety experts who write long reports explaining why the railroad was at fault in causing accidents and injuries. Expert reports like these get the railroad's attention.

Next, the railroad owes you money based on the 'total damages' you suffered. The 'total damages' you suffered directly relate to your medical treatment and testing to prove the injuries you suffered. If your railroad has delayed or refused to allow you to have testing done, or sent you to a doctor who is slow to find out what injuries you suffered, you won't have any medical evidence to show what injuries you suffered. You can say all you want 'my back still hurts….' Or 'my neck hurts and the doctor never looked at it….' But if there is no test to show what injury you have, the railroad wins, and they will low ball your settlement. Our office routinely arranges for excellent medical treatment and testing for our clients so that the full extent of their injuries can be determined and they won't be shorted in their settlement or in court.

In a similar way, if you can't prove your medical injuries with doctor reports or testimony, then you will have a hard time arguing that you are entitled to any lost wages. We routinely hire an economic expert to calculate the full value of our clients' loss of past and future lost wages and benefits if their injuries keep them from returning to work. This economist will write a lengthy report outlining the current value of all such losses for you. This report, just like the report of the safety expert, gets the railroad's attention. They now have two experts they would have to face in court if they are not serious about resolving your claim and if they do not offer fair money for you. To be blunt about it, this is how you get a good, solid settlement for your railroad claim…not by hoping the railroad claims department will treat you fairly after your injury. [see chart on next page.]

Railroad injured workers need to remember that the claims department is a sophisticated entity of the railroad, whose primary goal is to make sure that railroad workers receive less for their injuries than what they should be receiving. While the claim agent may tell you it's going to be a quicker process to deal directly with him or her, we can tell you that what they're willing to pay is going to be less than the true value of your claim. The railroad claims agent is trying to pay as little as possible to settle the claim and does not have your best interests in mind.

While dealing with an experienced railroad attorney may take longer to resolve your claim, at the end of the day, it will be the

WWW.POOLSONODEN.COM

Which Railroad Worker Do You Think Will Get a Higher Settlement?

- ✗ No court claim filed means no pressure on railroad - if your claim doesn't settle, it doesn't matter to them.
- ✗ Railroad may hold key documents you will never know about - they have an advantage of knowing a lot more than you do about your accident.
- ✗ Railroad won't face any expert to say they caused your accident - they can simply deny they did anything wrong and blame it all on you.
- ✗ Railroad has controlled and probably limited your medical treatment - some of your injuries may have gone undiagnosed, which is just fine for the railroad.
- ✗ Railroad can argue you won't have any real lost wages, so your claim isn't worth much. If you claim lost wages, you may hear back 'well ... how are you going to prove that?'

- OR -

- ✓ You have pressure on railroad to be fair in settlement since trial date is pending in court.
- ✓ You have the ability to get key documents to prove the railroad was at fault.
- ✓ You have a safety expert that will testify against railroad in court if railroad doesn't settle.
- ✓ You have expert, non-company doctors who have performed tests and can explain what injuries you suffered and what that means for your future.
- ✓ You have an economist who will explain your list wages in court if railroad doesn't settle.

true value of your claim instead of what the claims agent decides is the minimal amount due to you after your injury. Even after paying attorney's fees on your claim, a good railroad attorney will increase the settlement value well beyond the attorney's fees of the claim. You hire experts when you buy and sell a house or when you seek good medical treatment that is important to you and your family. In a similar way, we encourage you to seek out the advice and help of a good railroad attorney when you are dealing with something as important as a serious work related injury that may affect you, and your family, for the rest of your life. Don't pay twice for your injury by trying to go it alone or with bad inexperienced legal advice.

RETURNING TO WORK AFTER AN INJURY CLAIM

Many workers ask us if merely filing a railroad claim means that they will not be allowed to return to work, regardless of their physical condition. They want to know 'If I am physically better after my injury, and can do the work of my old job, can I go back to the railroad?' The answer is yes. The railroad cannot stop you from trying to return to your former position after your doctors have cleared you to return to work. When you are injured, the railroad must mark you off as "on-duty injury." You do not lose your seniority rights while you are marked off as injured. If you are able to return to work, and if the railroad tries to prevent you from marking up or taking a return-to-work physical, it is a violation of the FRSA whistleblower statute. For example, I have a client who was an Amtrak engineer who was hurt on the job. She was off of work for almost two years, treating for her injuries. We were able to resolve her claim against the trucking company and the railroad, and she worked very hard to return to the career that she loved – driving trains. When she attempted to mark back up for work after her doctor had released her to full duty, the railroad would not allow her to take a return to work physical.

    After trying her case, the court agreed with us that not allowing her to take a return to work physical was a violation of the whistleblower statute because the railroad cannot interfere with a doctor's recommendation for either staying off of work or being able to return to work. My client was allowed to return to her job as a locomotive engineer with her full seniority rights and was awarded punitive damages as a punishment to the railroad for violating her whistleblower rights. To listen to this engineer tell more about her story, please visit our website at www.poolsonoden.com. Again, having a lawyer who understands the differences in the laws that cover railroad workers and how the injury law can work with the whistleblower law is very important, especially when an injured worker is attempting to return to work. Many clients ask us if they are able to return to work will they have a target on their back with the railroad. Unfortunately I've seen in many cases that the railroad attempts to retaliate against employees when they return to work.

This is the exact reason that in 2008 OSHA decided to extend whistleblower protection to railroad workers. So in the event that you are able to return to work and do not have a career-ending injury, it is important to document how the railroad supervisors and managers treat you when you return to work. For example, if for your entire career you've had minimal discipline, and you returned to work, and you start to receive numerous rule violations, it is important to talk to an attorney about your rights at that time. The railroad may be attempting to pad your personnel file, in order to terminate you after a second or third offense. The problem for the railroad is that if they are retaliating against you because of the personal injury that you had sustained, this is a violation of a whistleblower statute.

Again, talk to your attorney because of the short time frame that there is to file a whistleblower statute claim after the adverse action. Remember it is only 180 days from the time of the adverse action. It is imperative to talk to an experienced railroad attorney to make sure that you do not miss your deadline to file a complaint.

After you're injured, your doctor may tell you that you can return to light-duty work. As you know, at the railroad there is no such thing as light-duty work. However, many railroads have programs that say that they can get you light-duty work where you can work outside of your craft to ease your financial concerns. However, returning to light-duty work without being cleared to full duty from your doctor may actually make it more difficult for you to get the benefits that you're entitled. It also may endanger your own health and the safety of your fellow employees if you're not able to return to your craft and return to full duty.

    Before you accept any "light-duty positions" with the railroad, please always make sure to talk to your FELA attorney about the consequences of this action and also to discuss these options with your doctor to make sure that he or she is totally aware of what light duty means at the railroad, especially considering that there are no light-duty positions available. The railroad cannot force you to return to work until you and your doctor have made a decision that is in the best interest of your health and what you're able to do. It is important that you tell your doctor exactly what is required of you in your job as a railroad worker. It is much different work than a lot of sedentary positions, meaning that at the railroad almost all the jobs are medium to heavy-duty positions.

    There are not many jobs which require a railroad worker to sit at a desk or not carry a significant amount of rule books or equipment at any point while they're working. Your doctor needs to be aware of these lifting requirements and in order to protect yourself and other workers, you should not be in a rush to return to work until you can fully fulfill the duties of your position. Again, always talk to a FELA injury attorney before making any decisions about returning to work so that you and your family are protected.

    The bottom line is that while in an ideal world you would be given every opportunity to return to work after your injury, and your railroad would welcome you with open arms, the reality is more complicated than that. If you know you have a serious injury and your doctor is reluctant to send you back to work, it is most often best to have him restrict you from railroad work and you can then maximize your settlement. This allows you to control your future. If you return to work you may always be looking over your shoulder wondering if today may be the day the railroad finds a reason to run you off.

FELA: FAQs:

1 **How long do I have to file a claim?**

The strictly legal answer is that for an on-the-job injury under the Federal Employers' Liability Act (FELA), you have 3 years to file a claim. For a whistleblower claim under the Federal Rail Safety Act (FRSA), you have 180 days from the time of the adverse action to bring an administrative claim with OSHA, the Occupational Safety and Health Administration. To learn what constitutes an adverse action under the whistleblower law, read below.

However….the sooner you bring your claim the much greater likelihood you will receive a higher settlement. The value of your settlement is driven by two things- showing that the railroad bears some or all responsibility for your injury, and proving your injury through solid medical evidence. The sooner you file your claim the sooner your attorneys can start to gather evidence to show why your injury happened, and the sooner you can get to medical providers who will actively try to seek out what injuries you may have suffered. This generally takes running tests and often company chosen doctors will delay or refuse to run such tests. Always remember that you can go to the doctor of your choice.

❷ Is FELA the same as worker's compensation?

No. Railroad workers have unique federal rights that are not the same as workers' compensation afforded to most other types of workers in the country. The cornerstone of FELA is the continuing duty of the railroad to provide its employees with a reasonably safe place to work at all times and at all places of employment. Do not believe the railroad claims agent when he/she tells you that you are just a "workers' comp case" and the only compensation the railroad owes you is your wages. Workers' Compensation benefits are usually a fixed amount and normally undercompensate an injured worker, as workers' compensation provides no compensation for pain and suffering and only partial wages. However, railroad workers injured on the job are entitled to damages such as past and future lost wages, pain and suffering, past and future medical expenses, past and future benefits, and loss of enjoyment of life.

3 **What should I do after an injury?**

a) The most important thing to do after an accident is to get the medical care that you need with your own doctors. You DO NOT have to see the railroad's "doctor" and you can pick the doctor of your choice. Seeing a company chosen doctor can be one of the worst decisions you make in regards to your claim. The reason is simple--to determine how badly injured you are, it takes running tests; a doctor that wants more business from a large railroad company will not want to run the bill up on that railroad company and he may be reluctant to recommend expensive tests for you. It's easier for him to just delay you and 'wait and watch' in the hopes you may get better, than to actively run expensive tests to make sure you know the full extent of your injuries.

b) Be sure you report your injury and fill out the personal injury report for your railroad employer. Please see our "Personal Injury Form Checklist" on how to fill out your personal injury form.

c) Do not give a statement to the claim's agent or any supervisor/manager until you have sought counsel from your lawyer or your union representative. <u>You are not legally required to give any type of recorded statement and when your railroad claims agent asks for one, this should raise a bright red flag—he is looking out for the railroad and not you!</u>

d) Try to write down and remember all of the details of your accident including any witnesses to the accident.

e) Remember to apply for Railroad Retirement Board sickness benefits and disability benefits you may have to help supplement your lost income while you are out injured.

f) Call your experienced railroad injury lawyers at Poolson Oden to confidentiality answer all your questions and concerns. There is no cost at all for just talking with us or meeting in person — we truly want to make sure you know your options and that you don't make a mistake in your claim.

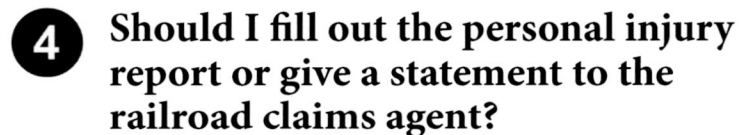

4 **Should I fill out the personal injury report or give a statement to the railroad claims agent?**

YES, you need to fill out your personal injury report as soon as possible after your injury as almost all railroads have rules that require their employees to fill this report out as close to the accident as possible. However, you do not have to fill out a personal injury report until you are capable in body and mind. This means that if you are in shock, pain, in the hospital undergoing treatment, taking medications that could affect your ability to competently fill out the report, you can agree to fill out the report as soon as you are ready. Please see our Personal Injury Form Checklist to help you fill out this vital report and contact your experienced FELA attorney as soon as possible for advice.

DO NOT give a statement to the railroad claims agent. There is nothing under the law that requires that you give a recorded or written statement to the railroad's claim agent.

5 **When should I hire an attorney and what kind of attorney do I need?**

You should seek legal advice from an experienced railroad lawyer as soon as possible after your accident. Because of the specialized nature of the laws covering railroad workers, you need a lawyer who knows these laws. You need a specialized railroad attorney who takes time to answer your questions for free. Call the attorneys at Poolson Oden to help you navigate these laws and keep your railroad claim on track.

6 **Do the railroads do surveillance of their injured employees?**

Yes, most of the time they do. The

railroads may become "peeping Toms" after your accident to try and "catch" you doing activities not consistent with your injuries. For example, if you have a back injury and are restricted to only lifting 10 pounds, the railroad wants to catch you at the store lifting a 20-pound bag of dog food. But while juries don't like "peeping Toms", they sometimes dislike dishonest people even more. The important thing to remember is to be truthful about any activities you are doing while you are injured and to document how you feel after doing activities in your daily life. You may be able to get the groceries or dog food into your car, but then may be in pain after. Be sure to follow the instructions of your doctor and if you have pain after certain daily activities, report them at your next appointment.

7 **What happens if the railroad blames me for my accident or injuries?**

Don't let the railroad claims agent tell you that if you were in any way responsible for your accident or injury, you will not be entitled to any compensation. FELA protects railroad workers, even if the worker is partially at fault. The FELA has a provision called "contributory negligence" which means that the railroad can still be held liable for your injuries even if they are only 1% at fault. If a jury would determine that you were partially responsible for your accident or injury, the jury could reduce the award you receive by the amount you are responsible. For example, if the jury awards you $500,000.00 and believes that you contributed 10% to your injury, then your claim would be reduced by $50,000.00.

8. The Vocational Rehabilitation program sounds helpful - why it is not!

The railroads like to offer "vocational rehabilitation services" to its injured employees. Vocational Rehabilitation typically is a program that provides training to help an injured individual return to his job or another job within his physical or mental restrictions. The railroad creates these "vocational rehabilitation programs" to offer jobs to injured workers within the company that are usually outside your craft and in another state. It is a smoke screen and is used at trial to make it appear that the railroad cares about its injured employees. At trial the railroad argues that it is the employees' fault that he or she is not back at work because they have offered jobs that the employee just wouldn't take. It is a sophisticated program that is not designed to help an injured worker. It is important that you speak with a FELA attorney to help you navigate the deceitfulness of these "helpful" programs.

9 **Do I have to get "approval" for my medical treatments through the railroad's "medical department?"**

No, you do not need approval to go to any doctor of your choice. The railroads prey on medical providers that are used to dealing with nurse case managers who work on claims for individuals covered under workers' compensation. Under the FELA, the railroad does not have a right to talk to your treating doctor, to have access to your medical records, or to be in the room when you are being examined by your doctor. The railroad processes your medical bills but these bills are processed under your group health insurance policy. Do not allow the railroad to talk to your doctors because they "pay the bills." As a railroad worker, you do not waive your doctor/patient privilege. This privilege is protected under the FELA and the whistleblower statute.

10. The Railroad always has to pay my wages when I get hurt, right? Wrong!

The FELA is a negligence-based statute. The railroad has a non-delegable duty to provide its employees with a safe place to work. In order to recover your wages and the other elements of damages in a FELA claim, it must be proven that the railroad failed to provide you with a safe place to work and that failure caused your damages, even in the slightest.

WWW.POOLSONODEN.COM

Whistleblower FRSA FAQs:

1 **What does "whistleblower" mean?**

A whistleblower in the railroad industry is an employee who is aware of his rights to have a safe work environment and who knows what to do to make the railroad responsible for failing to provide that safety.

2 **Am I protected from retaliation as a railroad worker?**

Yes. All railroad workers are protected by the Federal Railroad Safety Act (FRSA) which was enacted to promote safety in all areas of railroad operations and to ensure that railroad employees engaging in certain protected activities under the Act could do so without the fear or threat of discrimination or retaliation from their railroad employer.

3 **What are "protected activities" under the FRSA?**

a). Injuries - notifying the railroad of

your own work-related injury or a co-workers work injury.

b). Safety concerns - reporting hazardous safety or security conditions; refusing to violate federal law relating to rail safety; refusing to use or reporting the use of unsafe railroad equipment, tracks or structures.

c). Medical treatment – for a work related injury, the railroad cannot deny, delay or interfere with medical treatment; for a work related medical condition, the railroad cannot discipline an employee for following the treating doctor's orders or treatment plan.

d). Fraud or waste of public funds - providing information regarding the fraud, waste or abuse of government funds connected to rail safety or security

④ What power does the whistleblower law have?

The FRSA is a "make whole remedy" which makes available the following remedies:

Power to force the railroad to:

1. Reinstate you with all your seniority rights;

2. Pay your back wages with interest;

3. Pay all your economic losses;

4. Pay emotional distress damages;

5. Pay attorney's fees and costs'

6. Pay front pay if the Court finds that it is not in your best interest to return you to your former position; and

7. Pay punitive damages up to $250,000.

❺ Timeframe for filing? 180 Days! So short!

Under the whistleblower statute, a railroad worker only has 180 days from the adverse action of the railroad to file an administrative claim with OSHA. So many potential clients come to us after their time has expired and their rights have run out. If you have reported a safety issue or personal injury and have experienced a letter of reprimand in your file, a suggestion not to report the personal injury, being charged with rule violations repeatedly to pad your file, or harassment, contact the experienced railroad attorneys at Poolson Oden so we can help you immediately and protect your rights.

6 **Is racial discrimination part of whistleblower protection?**

No, the whistleblower statute protects railroad workers in areas of safety. The Equal Employment Opportunity Commission (EEOC) protects employees against racial discrimination.

WWW.POOLSONODEN.COM

FINAL THOUGHTS

It's About You and Your Family, Not the Railroad

After having helped injured railroad workers for more than 17 years we fully understand that many injured railroad workers just want to get back to work. They trust the railroad and believe what the claims agent tells them. Unfortunately, this can very often lead to unfair settlements and still injured railroad workers out there on their own struggling to find work.

We often ask those who come in and meet with us to discuss their situation, "If you had to go in off the street now and find work, could you get a decent job? Would you be able to pass a pre-employment physical or would a recent MRI show a back or neck problem that hasn't been resolved? What company would hire you now in the shape you are in?" The point is to take your railroad out of the equation—ask yourself, if you find yourself on your own, and you need to knock on doors to find work, how successful do you think you will be? That type of hard self-reflection usually helps our clients see their situation more realistically. Often, it's our clients' spouses or family members who first see the situation for what it is—they are often the ones who will encourage our clients to come meet with us.

We encourage you to phone us or visit with us in person so we can discuss your situation. Railroad cases are complex, and your case is extremely important to you. Waiting until you 'have to' make a decision very often limits your best outcomes. The time to make important decisions is when you have the most options still open to you. With a railroad injury claim, this is usually right after your accident occurs.

POOLSON | ODEN
RAILROAD & SERIOUS INJURY ATTORNEYS

About Poolson Oden — The law firm of Poolson Oden focuses on helping injured railroad workers. Second only to their own families, they view their clients as real family and find fulfillment and meaning in protecting the rights of every injured railroad worker. In a time when many people fear hiring an attorney, Danny and Carisa find joy in connecting with their clients and putting them at ease as they help lead their clients to their best future possible after their injuries.

Danny Poolson — Following law school, Danny was honored to serve as a Judicial Law Clerk to the Honorable Marilyn Castle, Chief Judge of the 15th Judicial District Court in Lafayette, Louisiana. As a State Court Law Clerk, he worked on complex litigation gaining valuable experience in several practice areas, including personal injury cases and insurance claim disputes. After practicing law for several years in Lafayette, Danny returned to New Orleans to practice law and contribute to the rebuilding of the city.

Danny is married to Amy D. Poolson of Opelousas, LA, and they are the proud parents of twins Davis Daniel and Amelia Isabella ("Twinkies"). When he is not working hard on his cases, Danny enjoys spending time with his family and traveling to see the LSU Tigers play.

Carisa German-Oden — Since earning her law degree, Carisa has represented injured railroad workers and their families throughout the country. Carisa has extensive litigation and trial experience in both state and federal court. Before she became a railroad attorney, Carisa worked at a law firm exclusively protecting the rights of railroad workers. In fact, in her extensive 17-year legal career, she has only represented injured individuals and injured railroaders working at a firm designated by the UTU, BLE and SMART TD unions.

Carisa and her husband Michael have three children, Abigail, Felix and Sebastian.

Made in the USA
Columbia, SC
28 December 2020